Goddess

of the

Edges

Elizabeth Carson

Dedication

To the wonderful women of my book club. You've been
my first audience and cheered me on in my poetic
endeavors. It wouldn't have happened without you.

Thanks especially to Iris and Mary Ann, who each
provided inspiration for one of the poems in this book.

Table of Contents

Goddess of the

Edges

Old Willis Point Road

Twenty years ago or so
they built new Willis Point Road:
    straighter, faster, wider,
      more convenient, more direct.

The old road ran through government land.
They cut it off with high and serious fences
    and left it to its untended fate.

It went fast.

Cracks and potholes opened the way to saplings.
The road greened itself, tarmac disappearing
    into woodland scrub.
With flowing, fragile might, the earth reclaimed
    the artificial imposition.

By now, I expect there's nothing much left
to remind us
    that once we thought we owned
    Old Willis Point Road.

The Old Ones at the Well

The well is in the center of the plaza
    at the center of the village.
No one remembers its history,
    or when it wasn't there.

In the near-dawn an old one appears,
as sturdy as the land.
    She carries a bowl.
    She goes to the well.
Within moments, she is joined
by generations of the old ones of the village
    bringing their bowls to the well.

No words are spoken or needed.
An invisible current connects them
to each other, to the well, the plaza, the village.

Then a sound, like faraway chant:
the old ones murmur in an ancient tongue,
    pull water from the well
    and dip their bowls.
Each sips, each sprinkles a few drops
    on the pavement of the plaza
    at the heart of the village.
They turn then, and vanish,
    as silently as they came.

The plaza glows with the colours of the sky.
The first person comes
    to draw from the life-giving well.
More come, all day, to the well on the plaza
    at the center of the village.

The water is clear, and sweet, and pure.

The Swans of Winter

(Every year the trumpeter swans return to
over-winter on Tod Creek Flats, behind the Red
Barn in Victoria.)

Potatoes grow on the Flats.
Throughout the summer they march in place,
in lines, green on brown.

In autumn, most years, the rains come
and the Flats becomes a pond
more grey than the winter sky.

Soon, soon...

I have seen this: Your hand
lightly cupped over the Flats
just above the height of a swan's flight.

Your grip loosens, Your hand turns,
And out they tumble,
one, three, ten,
the sky a blizzard of swans.

Awkward at first,
they right themselves, stretch,
fly in lazy loops,
descend to the water.

The trumpeters have returned.

All winter I watch them
in stately formation through water and air,
sailing wedges of white on grey,

until March – they take wing,
    circle a final salute,
turn Arctic-bound.

The Flats drains, grows potatoes,
    in lines, green on brown.

The Beggar

It's not the menace implied by your presence
that freezes me in place,
not the black under your nails, dirt
        ground into the hand you hold out.
It's not the ratty beard framing the bloodshot eyes
or the filthy clothes that hang on your thin frame,
or the stubs of teeth.
It's none of these things.

Or all.

Because it's the sum of what you are
that bludgeons me.

You stop me short, undeniable
        in a brief, unwelcome meeting of eyes,
        to fumble awkwardly for change.
Stark, immediate, challenging
        my well-dressed assumptions
        about a day in the city.

My reaction is primal, not logical.
Because you are not logical,
        you are so damned immediate.
And I am pinioned by the truth
of where this leaves me.

If you are reality,
then I am a china doll.

On Faith

Only watch: the clear and pure focus of the child
raising her palms skyward
to bless the soul of her fallen pet,
complete in her assurance
that her blessing will matter,
and is holy.

Goddess of the Edges

Goddess of the edges of the day,
trailing coral scarves across a dusky sky,
your hair awash in amethyst,
your shoes all aflame –
not for you the hard edges of light,
the expected doubts of darkness.

Yours is the changing time,
where gradients are guides, and insights appear
from shadow.

Yours the reflection and the silhouette,
yours the mist that wraps the field,
the melding of sky's boundary with sea.
Yours the unknown of beginnings,
the softening of endings.
Yours the flickering beacon light
on the path
to the unclaimed future.

Doze

Again.
I drag my stone-heavy
    head back to vertical,
drag open drowsy eyes
    from their irresistible Yes of closing.

Think about acquiring:
    a less cozy chair,
    a less welcoming fire,
    a less lazy afternoon.

It's a good book, this;
it's in no hurry to be finished.

Lament for Mary

Did you know, when the angel came,
what you were buying into?
Did you know that you would be
a sacrificial lamb,
as much as ever that famous son of yours was?

He left his father's way,
this first-born miracle son.
Rejected you and your gentle words,
set himself on a personal path to destruction.

Your son had a choice of destiny,
though he perhaps denied it.
God chose yours.

When He sent the angel,
designating you to bear this son,
did He not know
that a mother, of all creation,
understands and is bound by love?

Downtown Ghosts

Someone got beaten up right here
on this street corner
last night.
Some other guy didn't like the way
he looked, or looked at.

There was blood.
People gathered to watch.
There was a siren.

But that was last night.
Today, a thousand well-shod feet walk over the place,
reclaiming the pavement.

No one looks, or looks at.
Probably don't even know about last night.
The ghosts seldom cross over
from that world to this.

Elder Walk

Wandering in a soft, persistent rain –
Shapes in the mist become cedar, Douglas fir.
The path is sheltered by bigleaf maple,
  caressed by ocean spray,
  punctured by sword fern.
The ocean whispers on the stony beach,
and the ancestors of this land are here.

Not my ancestors; I have no claim
  to their wisdom.
But I feel their presence.

There is a rightness in the afternoon,
a fitting cover to the land.
It has been this way since the times before time,
  horizon obscured,
  boughs dripping in soft rhythm,
  hints of myth in the voice of raven ...

Not my ancestors, no.
but even so, I know this:
  they are watching.
Oh, yes.
They are here. They know.
Guides or judges,
  they are watching.

Dig

Dig.
Dig deep beneath the foundations,
Dig furiously with sweat and blisters,
    shovel and pick and bloodied nails.

Dig until daylight gains no purchase
    on the walls of the prison shaft.
Dig until contact is lost and you are alone,
    entombed by your digging.

Dig down to the bedrock, then stand and feel it shake
    as the earth rebounds.
    Break through, and dig.

Dig past pain and disbelief.
Dig until you're scorched by the core of raging fire,
    searing you down to the essentials.

Dig.
Dig until the earth cracks open
onto a vast interior,
and a bridge across the chasms of everyday
    draws you to the undefined horizon
    and cool blue mists
    caress your burning eyes and feet

and you can see at last
from a place beyond the digging,
    your truth, and
    the limitless sky.

Cold, Empty Bed

The songs have it wrong.

I'm not interested in the
    cold, empty place in the bed
    now that he's gone.
Even as metaphor,
    a bed fails to get at
    the depth of it.

Maybe it's just that
I am not a young woman.
"Now that he's gone" has a different meaning, now.

So how about:
    The sky has been emptied of birds.
    Nothing can take flight, nothing sings
    except the raven, with his song of doom.

How about:
    A killer frost decimated the garden,
    glazed the paths, now too dangerous
    for walking.

How about:
    There's a silence, that for a lifetime
    was the quiet of a heartbeat, a barely heard breath,
    a page turning.

How about:
        Who, in this new, scary silence
        shall I tell about the sky and the birds?
        Who will lament with me
                the fuchsia and the marigold?
        Who will take my hand, steady me
        as I walk down the long, long path?

Rescue Kitten (Terra #1)

Three days it took,
you, guarded and hurting, on my lap,
before you thought it would be all right.

You, before:
 at the mercy of first-time hormones,
lost on the winter streets,
abandoned and imprisoned,
        waiting, waiting...
surgery and pain, strange hands,
and the final indignity, a head cold.

No wonder you were frightened.
No wonder my lap became your refuge.

Now, now you remember
        how to chase balls, demand food,
        stretch and roll,
        sleep on your back by the fire.

But still I see,
        in the way you wait
        patiently at the door,
the fear that I won't be there,
the relief, in fervid rubs and purrs, when I am.

And for me, equal fear:
your life in my keeping,
the weight of it almost greater
than the joy.

High Road to Heaven

They speak of a high road to Heaven,
    and warn that it's narrow and tough,
    with penalties for falling off,
    and no guarantees.

But just suppose
    that you build that road yourself
    whenever you think or say or do.

And suppose
    that the smooth bits
    are respite for the rocky bits,
    but both are meant to be there,
    not as penalties and rewards,
    but simply because that's how life dealt them.

And suppose
    that even where it's tough going,
    the guard rails are sturdy,
    and you know you can't fall off.

And suppose
    that as you climb, the skies dance above you
    and the breezes soothe,
    the sun laughs and hosannas are sung
    and palms lay themselves down at your feet.

And suppose
    that the path only goes
    as far as you've created it, so far.
    And as far as you've created it,
    that's Heaven.

Seascape

The Tasman's mad today;
grey tide whispers seething down the beach.

The Tasman menaces.

Restive West Coast gods have
something on their minds,
    throwing used-wash-water foam like this
    across wet-shiny stones,
    beer-bottle glass,
    detritus of the sea.

Clear enough, the voice
    of those who got here first.

This faith presumes no scripture,
and I wonder, could it be
    that Galilean gods were elemental once,
    and spoke with this directness?

Charlie

Charlie loves us,
yappy little ginger thing in her green plaid sweater,
planting wet paws on my jeans
whenever we meet.
Charlie dances on her hind legs,
overcome with the joy
of walks and smells and people.

Charlie's mistress grips the short leash.
Far too thin after the surgeries,
she welcomes a pause to rest,
a neighbourly chat in the afternoon sun.

They move slowly together
down the sidewalk,
complementary energies,
neither able
to run free.

Tea Party

It's relatively minor, but
they're going to knock you out.
Powerless in the alien bed,
mind and body prepped for surgery,
you're told,
  so sorry, there's a delay.

Several hours more to wait,
no food or drink
since the night before.

By the time they come for you
you don't care what they do.
Famine has overpowered fear.

When you wake up in your room, it's night.
A nurse says, I shouldn't do this –
and conjures up hot, sweet, milky tea,
toast with raspberry jam.

Manna never tasted so good.
Saints walk the earth.
You sleep, repaired.

At the Cathedral

The craft of poetry finds its place, among other crafts,
in a stained glass window in the cathedral downtown.
There's a saint, but better, a scribe,
for what is poetry but the shaping of truth by craft?

The cathedral's own truths meet the world
as stone and ritual,
container and contents spilling over,
words and rhythm crafted for travel beyond the walls,
    as if the structure can't contain
    the fullness of it, the power.

Cathedral poetry is real, though perhaps not real-world.
Because it's almost too much for words, this poetry.
The alchemy of worship reshapes ritual,
just as the stained glass window shatters
    the incoming light,
the saint and the scribe remade
into new patterns on the floor,
    born from illumination beyond the stone,
    testing the words
    that try, and fail, to say it all.

The Stag
(The Poet Meets the King)

Last night's sprinkle lives on
    in muddy jeans,
      sodden fingers of cotton gloves.
One more weed, one more deadhead,
stand and ease my back.
Up and down the driveway bed, things look good.

That's when I see him
motionless, head erect
beside the garage.

My drive is the Royal Road.
Around me rises the whisper:
the King, the King ...
    or could it be the wind in the firs?

He takes his first proud step, pauses.
The heralds advance,
their gilt banners pendant from sounding horns ...
    or could it be the sun among the shadows,
    the crow in the maple?

This is a breath-holding moment.
Never have I seen
such antlers, such a crown.

Another step and another, the procession has begun.
He stops to accept a floral tribute, moves on.

As he draws near we brush eyes;
he pays no attention to a humble subject.
I hear the rustle of crinoline as I curtsey ...
        or could it be the crunch of hooves on the gravel?

At the end of the drive he pauses, turns right.
I lose him in the throngs of garden.
The drive lies still in the summer sun,
touched by majesty.

Approaching Solstice (Winter)

Arrive naked.
Strip yourself of ornament and expectation.

But should your courage fail,
brace yourself to molt,
    the old shell fallen away
    to leave you fertile and fearful.

The carapace
will no longer serve.

Do not go prepared,
do not bring lists or resolutions.

Instead, listen beyond the boundaries.
Allow yourself to hear what you know
    as the pull of yearning long denied
    moves you into flood tide, moon tide,
    sunset.

The old patterns
no longer serve.

Go humble and opened,
with only the gentlest touch
as from an ancestor's hand on your shoulder
    to remind you
    where you started,

to remind you
why you came.

Squall on the Bog

The squall runs over the bog in waves,
shaped by the wind into peaks and troughs;
five minutes later
the sun dries everything out in waves of steam.

If nothing is forever, at least it's all in order.
I am reminded once again
    that squalls, like sun, happen;
    that where there is water, there is also fire;
    that one treats with rainbows
    only through rain.

Short Story

Her flight was one with darkness, yet
first light revealed
the swath her skirt cut in the dew.

From a high window his eyes pursued
her trail, until it merged with lingering night.
With shadowed thoughts, he went downstairs

to wait. A light low mist washed down
to shroud the field, the dawn – and her,
seeking alone what was never there

for her, with him. And yet ...
                              if she came back,
his time come, he would usurp
the dilatory Sun, himself repair

what damage morning chill had done.
A quiet, calming warmth was his,
a flame subdued

and steady, though her captured spirit crave
such passion bursting now beside the earth,
Hurling daylight through the air.

Cyclamen

The cyclamen by the sink
is birthing a flower.

A ragged business, this,
each petal on its own, in its own time,
fighting its own battle to vertical
through leaves and stems and gravity.

By tomorrow, the next day at the latest,
the calyx will be well sheltered,
leaving undefended the circular opening below,
an open treasure chest.

Easter

Resurrection, that's not the miracle.
Incarnation's the true miracle,
and never mind who's calling whom
        a god.

And once incarnate,
once safely embodied,
who can say what isn't now a miracle.
Anything at all?
The human container serves a purpose,
until its time is done.
Its fate, once emptied,
is really neither here nor there.

In the meantime,
the only proper stance is amazement,
the only suitable response
to every living hour
        is awe.

Reading the Writer

Sit down, peruse
a paragraph at random, any book will do.
And think about the words
that someone else's muse
dictated to the page,
and so, through some unlikely chance,
to you.

This is a gift, these thoughts, these views,
in rhythm with your private dance,
or alien and new.
How likelier it was to never choose
this paragraph in front of you.

But choose you did, and now
you can't undo.
The words acquire a mental glue,
they challenge or enhance,
clarify or confuse.

The choice is yours:
discount, or use.

The Dead Crow

The crow's wing lay splayed
    across the dirty dead snow.

Feathers dull and tattered, this crow
had survived sun and storm,
barbs and battles –
    until now.
He stood no chance against the triple threat
of age, hunger, cold.

Whatever. The next snow
will bury his defeat, there on his frigid bed.
With spring melt he'll be gone.

He's done his bit, this crow.
Memory's talons cling,
then release into April.
The crows that remain have noticed,
    and flown,
        and remember no more.

I Will Spin a Prayer

I will spin a prayer this night
as a thread of gold and silver,
flying away from the spindle of my heart
to You my Lady, somewhere beyond the stars.

Somewhere? I know where.
Haven't You told me ceaselessly,
sending Your voice through a thread
of gold and silver?

The end doubles back, weaves into my soul
with messages of Sophia.

Here is the heart of mystery.
The secret lies within, bound up by my spinning,
ever spinning,
threads of gold and silver.

The Unknown (Terra #2)

I carry her sprawling
    from her fire-toasted doze.

"Terra – look."

On the window ledge,
sitting precisely, tail tucked just so,
Terra looks.

The view she knows so well
is now incomprehensibly alien.

Unable to explore or understand,
Terra rewards the still-falling snow
with a querulous, dismissive
three-syllabled Miaow

and takes herself off to what is certain:
    the carpet, the fire,
    chin resting on tail,
    the occasional twitch
    as she dreams the snow.

Petunias

The petunias want watering.

I'm neglecting them now,
    out of place, a summer flower
    stranded in the season of gold.

They're called Bubble Gum.
It's breathtaking, the way they're going
    exuberantly into autumn,
not catching the signals, what's coming
    to cut them down.
Going with such flamboyance, such *pinkness*
    in the face of muted browns and yellows.

I'm surely in the golden season
    (though not clad in shades of Bubble Gum).
In deeper attunement than petunias, I store my sap,
    batten down.
When frost obliterates their brilliance,
I will be in stasis, snug and smug …

but perhaps with something lacking,
    some touch of outrageous,
    some daring unseasonality,
    some bright defiance in the face of
    summer's end.

Urban Bog

The shore pines are dying,
out in the middle of the bog.
They date from another era,
when this land earned money
for some farmer.

I wonder if we should even call it natural, now.
A weir controls this soggy bit of pseudo-wildland.
Man-God decides if it's to be bog
or potato patch.

Well, the ducks and coots don't care.
They hang out on the water,
raise their broods in the cattails,
congregate where the people are
        (the people with the bread crumbs),

while the red tail hawk sits sentinel,
and the red wing blackbird rains down
        his liquid notes of benediction.

In the Garden

O Eve, did you ever taste
    the sweets of the garden,
    once you knew what you had?
Or were you too frightened
    by those footsteps on the path,
    expecting the condemnation they carried?

And once you were out, and the gates were closed,
    did you really regret?
Or did you find in your new awareness
    a fine counterbalance
    to what you were told was lost?

Eden could only be a fool's paradise, you know,
    untouched by anything truly alive.
The walls sheltered you, but kept you
    in the haze of illusion; kept you unborn,
    barred from the threshold into life.

I think you made a good bargain, there under the tree.
Reality beats dreaming your life away.
You dared the fruit, your legacy is freedom.
    Now we your children taste it all,
    now we dare to call you goddess.

Letting Go

Life bears a heavy debt to death.

When revelation speaks as breaking,
free it!
Let attachment cease!
And in the practice, gradually
    release
        your hold

on life's uptakings and bestowings,
a partial payment to the greater knowing –
and thus reduce the balance owing.

Until, when you join that finer peace,
connecting at last the first and final breath,

The balance,
chipped away in slow outflowing

allows a gentler going.

Dance

The body's grown stiff, following its routine,
    behaving itself, like an adult.

But remember?
Put on Glen Miller, Elvis,
    Beach Boys, Beatles,
    Creedence.
Your muscles remember those days, those rhythms.

And the guy...
the one whose shadowy, imagined face filled your head,
    who danced you around your bedroom floor
    while your parents complained about the noise
    and privately wondered why you were alone
        on a Saturday night.

Remember him?

Did you think he had forgotten you?

No one is home; the night is young.
Put on the music, summon him forth,
Dance.

Breakfast (Misty #1)

Bewhiskered one glares up indignant-eyed.
  What?? Dry food for breakfast?
Spurns warm milk, a pitiful appeal
To half-remembered kitten-days.

  Give me tuna, gravy of beef,
  Chicken and halibut, table scraps at least!

Bewhiskered one glowers, and won't be loved;
Stalks off with proud-held tail,
Gazes rapt in carrion dreams –

While just outside the window
Fat thrushes sing good morning.

The First Five Minutes

When there's still a choice.
When fear is gone, and
        curiosity kicks in.
When the damned pain
        evaporates,
and no one's expectations matter.

Most likely you'll stay,
        but it's not airtight.
Most likely, if you're sent back
        (they do say it can happen)
        you won't be best pleased.
Attachments melt in this new perspective:
        the spouse, the dog, the new sofa,
        the kids, the fancy coffee maker,
        the symphony, book club, choir...

In the first five minutes you can still go back.
But now you have to deal with what's true,
because there's no pretending any more.

Fruition

A plump, red apple poses on the counter,
red as life, flaunting its redness
        in a patch of autumn sun.

A dozen apples, bursting with summer.

In a soft, golden day, I ripen like apples ...

Ripen into thoughts of
        the mystery of
        the exquisite alchemy of

                autumn

                apple

                pie.

When apples dream of ripening
they dream of pie:
        Summer's culmination,
        peak of aspiration,
        October fruits' ordained fruition.

Albino Crow

I always imagined there was something between us,
    some special awareness,
though in fact I never touched her.
She'd preen her whiteness
    in the window of the pet store,
and I'd be there, on the other side of the glass,
    watching.

They say she had a happy life –
large space and food, games to challenge her,
    warmth and no rain.

She wouldn't have survived,
    living as nature intended.
    Disliking differences, the other crows
    would have seen to that.
So her prison was the better bet.
It's not just a lack of tools or skills
    that kills you.

I asked once, and the pet store gave me
    three molted feathers.
Now among my treasured things –
a gift from my sister.

Change (Terra #3)

Today we re-arranged
    the furniture,
added a table tennis table,
moved her bowls to a new location.

She is tired tonight,
    missed her afternoon nap,
    suspiciously watching
    the goings-on.

She'd rather not be left alone
in this newly strange room.

Thursday Afternoon

Tyler tripped Ashley up
going home from school today.
Stuck-up, stupid Ashley, thinks she's so much
     better'n us.
Serves her right, dumbass bitch.

And boy, did she put on a show –
about how horrid we are and gonna tell her dad,
     like we care about *him*.
Thought she'd pee herself, down on the ground,
her face all dirty and snotty,
hole in her sweater where her elbow hit.

That'll teach her.
Justin dumped her schoolbag, homework blew away,
     then we ran.
Grabbed some cookies, shot goals on the driveway,
and Mom made pot roast for supper.

Summer City Weekend

You squeeze the oranges
while I start the perk
and bring out soft new napkins.

Two perfect apples
a fine old cheddar
croissants made crunchy in the oven.

On the tray I put
a vase with the dahlias
we bought at the Saturday market.

Our deck looks out over the city
still sleeping, but the sun is full
and the day is yellow.

No hurry to this breakfast, we have
all Sunday to talk and wander;
claiming the weekend.

Left

Once they stood on docks
    and watched their children go
    to a life beyond conceiving.
Once, mothers wrung their hands,
hands that would never again touch
    a cheek,
    an errant lock of hair,
hands that would never cradle the next generation.

Leaving was forever, once.

Now, we leave, we modern children,
    and how far is it, after all?
Phone calls, texting, Skype:
    we're just around the global corner.
We're in touch,
it's how it is,
it has to be enough.

Until the day
when we're the parents on the dock.
And, too late, we get it –
    the hollow longing in the hand
    through long years
    of never touching, never cradling
    the child.

Leaving was forever, once.
And now we understand ... it still is.

What's Hidden

There is a woman – you know her,
we all know her –
whose days are shaped,
like all of our days,
by self-selected fences.

Kitchen and car,
        family and work,
A million expectations, others' and her own.
Her life. Our lives.

Her family sees her, there at the sink,
gloved hands lost in suds.
We all see her.

And yet somehow we miss ...

... how she stands
alone on a treeless hill
her hair caught by the wind,
with no witness but the moon.

Again the song she learned with first blood
arises in her heart and releases
to fertilize the earth.

In regal solitude,
her arms raised,
her voice a living thing,
she cries her song to the heavens.

and flies home.

Iris Reads Poetry

Poetry is self-indulgence.
The poet spews thoughts of deep profundity
in magnificent gusts of grandiloquent words,
writhing snakes of sentences, images
    punctuation

       and line

        breaks
presumably meaningful to the poet,
such that ordinary mortals say huh?
and graduate students write dissertations
in arcane language
understood by the select few,
their own superior insights
fuel for the poet's vanity.

A Little Spring Song

Dance to the dogwood,
curtsy to the clover,
celebrate the new grass,
caper in the rain.
Blessed by the warming,
under heaven's turning,
dawn of earth's evolving,
living again.

Love in the springtime
blossoms in the moment.
To April's imperatives
ever be true!
Bluebirds are mating –
why ever are we waiting?
Life's recreating
Eden anew.

Winter Solstice 2011

Begin in dark,
    For everything is born in dark:
the fire a spent bed of embers,
the candle guttered,
the cards read, the bones cast.

And now...
        clouds battle the near extinguished moon,
        chill winds press fingers to your cheek,
        lift your hair,
        an owl shrieks somewhere, out there.

Now, the waiting...

The dark lives, not yet in retreat,
reminding those who listen
        that tonight is the night for seeing,
        the night that gives an opening
        to the dreams of tomorrow.

On Distraction

Damned raucous birds! Intentioned as they are
to shatter peace with bursts of merriement,
their trills provoke, much to the detriment
of solemn thought; frivolitie to jar
and grate upon the melancholie ear
which, seeking only fresh presentiment
of miserie, in bitter love's lament,
the heart from cheerful melodie would bar.

Fain would I withdraw from pleasure sweet
and spurn these winged sprites that me entreat
to sacrifice despair to lively cheer.
Away with them! And leave me to the drear
of love thus unreturned, that all may see
I sup on daily draughts of misery.

Lauds

The hour fills my mind
as water from a sacred well
fills a chalice.

There should be bells,
ringing across hills that awaken
to the unformed promise of an unknown day.

Light celebrates its own creation,
a slow rebirth as grays dissolve
and the world receives the gift
in palpable stillness.

Laud and magnify this numinous time,
when potential limns the landscape
and tendrils of blessing escape into the dawn.

Sip from the chalice, resonate with the bells,
set the path with praise.
Follow the untouched day where it will go.

Payment

You pay your money, and
>   the poor get Christmas,
>   a donkey lives safe for a year,
>   a village gets water to drink,
>   a street person gets socks.

Curled up by the fire, you watch the cold rain
and plan
>   this week's menus
>   the night at the opera,
>   a spa day with friends,
>   your winter wardrobe.

You write the cheques,
and you feel so, so good.

Approaching Solstice (Summer)

They say …
    that if at dawn, you gaze
    into the standing water in a stump
    you will see the face of the one
    you are to marry.
The earth will dance for you, this day,
the very rocks will sing your power.

They say …
    you must wash your face in the morning dew
    to assure a fine complexion
    to lure the one you love.
Look to the waters to store and carry
transforming energy.
Trust it, for it is sparely offered
    and the time is short.

The shift has begun.
Seize the light while you can,
    and read the omens.
Soon enough the long shift into darkness
    will begin.

Doors #2

(Inspired by *The Elegance of the Hedgehog*)

An open door disturbs
whatever lies beyond,
an alien form
intruding upon the space:
not the transition,
not the furnishing.

No wonder we push into rooms
without the respect due to the passage
from one reality
to the next.

But allow a door to slide
into a pocket in the wall
and all is simple and proper.
The new room waits inviolate;
the door, neither here nor there,
honours its role
and retains the mystery
of the boundary.

Bookmobile

You'd see it drive up,
a lumbering ship of possibility –
but everything hung suspended while
the older kids went first.

Out in the parking lot
you had to wait in line,
so afraid the first to go in
would get all the good books.

They didn't, of course.

You'd choose your limit,
within five minutes or so;
hand over your card,
watch the stamp on the slips.
And then they were yours,
two weeks of treasure claimed.
You'd climb down the stairs
to the real world, giddy
with magic
in your arms.

Now it's IPads and texting;
the bookmobiles are going
or gone.

Can Twitter tweet the same anticipation?
I trust, in the name of magic,
that something's salvaged of that childhood world,
that the bookmobile, in different form,
lives on.

The Scent of Things

Lilacs

Seductress!
You lure me from my path through enchantment,
     every time.
It seems I can't do without you, especially now,
     in the dawning of summer.
But if I take you,
     you die in a day.
Your allure is strong but your substance is weak,
     your loyalty up for question,
       your commitment not to be trusted.

Laurel

Popsicles, lollipops –
one whiff and it's a childhood day in summer,
the best kind, of freedom and ice cream and sun.
And yet, when I approach you,
     there's no reward. You withhold your flavour
     from the inquiring nose.
It's only when an errant breeze wanders
across the pond,
     hopscotching over the fence
     to touch your blooms,
that the air rewards me with memory.

Skunk Cabbage

How fortunate, that you're milder
        than your namesake.
Even so, you fill the valley;
admiring your brazen bracts
        is a pungent act.
I like the reminder,
        the natural nature of your scent
        that refuses to be beautiful,
        that says take me or leave me,
        that stands on its own.

Crow Wisdom

It came as a bright bauble
dropped into my hand
from the moving midnight blackness above me.

I cast it away
for its flashiness,
its *commonness*,
its lack of subtlety,
     sophistication,
     mystery.

But crow was having none of that.
Time and again she returned the gaudy thing
     (as crows will do),
dropping it into my hand, saying
     Pay
     Attention.
Until at last I looked.

And beneath the glitz,
lay all I had forgotten.

Crow's wisdom is never subtle sophisticated mysterious.

Crow's wisdom is:
>You are here, now.
>You have nowhere better to be.
>You have been given the rare gift
>of being alive:
>>flashily,
>>commonly,
>>*alive.*

What, for heaven's sake
(and crows are masters of exasperation)
are you waiting for?

It's given, time and again,
dropped into your hand,
until you see.

Summer City Night

To be in a room in the city,
jazz on the radio, and Saturday night.

Alone.

The longing that moves in the night is for
      nothing that ever was,
and for nothing that could be –
but always has been, and cannot end.

The heart has knowledge of what
      daytime keeps at bay:
this isn't sadness, or loss, but an odd, lonely content.

This is a summer city night,
      alone with jazz on the radio,
paying homage to the essential separation,
not seeking a remedy, but opening to
the impossible solitude of being.

Green Cotton Bag (Terra #5)

Terra's asleep on a green cotton bag,
its handle looped around her body,
her head tucked into a fold.
The scrunched-up fabric is her self-designated place
in a world so much bigger than she is.

It's not a bad idea, really,
that we, each of us, get to choose
a green bag,
with a handle to hold us snug,
a fold to hide in.

Persephone

Untried as you were, how could you know
    what fate awaited you?
Virgin daughter, free in the fields,
the world your playground –
still a seed of your mother, your own power
    lay dormant, unsuspected.

Nothing could have prepared you
for that thunderbolt awakening.
The black chariot stole you from innocence
to destiny, awoke you from the dream.

What might now is yours, oh Persephone!
Men quail before you, for the dreaded Underworld,
    home of all secrets and fears,
    is yours.
Men celebrate your return to the garden,
for the prospering of the earth
    is yours.

Never underestimate
a woman's awakening.
There's no turning back; once the black chariot
    shows her the way to her self,
she is forever
made Goddess.

New Year 2010

New Year's Day dawned luminous,
you might say iridescent.
The sun was undefined, barely brighter than the sky.
It was as if the air might birth, at any moment,
a blizzard of rainbows against the opal morning.

So still it was,
drops hung suspended from red berries,
just as the day seemed suspended,
not yet fully realized.
Possibility quivered alive in the hazy light,
the veiled promise of a new cycle.

I walked, and the world slept.

And there on top of the bare oak tree,
a Cooper's hawk – perched motionless
as time held its breath.
His tail flared,
he surveyed the future
through the soft almost-mist.

About Cupcakes

They show themselves so prettily,
there in tidy rows,
each immaculate cake identical to the next,
right down to the swirl in the icing,
like perfectly matched little jewels.

Like little pretenders, you mean.
Let me tell you about cupcakes.

They begin in the mixer, rotating away
while you scrape the bowl.
When the batter's ready, lick the beaters –
      just to be sure they'll be good.
Pour into rainbow cups your mother bought just for you,
      two-thirds full – well, more or less.

While they bake, lick the bowl.
With fingers to get it all.

You have to wait while they cool.
But there's icing to be sampled …

Then spread whatever icing's left like putty,
      filling in the hollows, thinner on the ridges,
      catching a few crumbs for texture.
Add sprinkles.
Add more sprinkles.

Line them up on the counter,
      short and tall, smooth and bumpy,
with random amounts of cake and icing and sprinkles,
and choose your cupcake.
Peel the rainbow paper
 and take that first bite.

Now, these are cupcakes to wear
      on your lips, your cheeks,
      your fingers and your shirt.
These are disorderly cupcakes,
      exuberantly, rambunctiously imperfect.
No regimented, jewel-like wannabes,
these, my dear,
are the real thing.

Cemetery Etiquette

Received etiquette says,
    Hush, walk sedately,
    Kneel.
Unspoken rules dictate
    an attitude of reverence,
    flowers at your resting place.

But when were you ever reverent?
There should be Frisbees, music and dancing,
as if you were really here to add
    a flying catch,
    a guitar riff with the band.

This silence ill becomes you.
Come, join the party,
play with me, as if to overcome
    what we both,
    in our different ways,
    have lost.

Walled Garden

I had a garden.
The stone walls guarded against invasion,
    the gate was thick old wood
    with a sturdy lock, and
    only I had the key.
Inside was quiet order:
    the formal paths all raked and smooth,
    ornamental petals and leaves just so.
No weeds dared grow.
A quiet, pensive place to be still
    and hear my voices.

One day a voice said,
    Leave the gate ajar.

I have a garden,
    and the gate is ajar.
Nothing is shaped, nothing is pruned.
Rampant, the honeysuckle scales the walls.
Carrots grow under the lavatera,
    wild flax rubs elbows with roses.
Birds fly in for the seeds and twigs,
    small animals rustle the undergrowth.
The flowers are blowsy, their petals carpet the beds.
The very pattern of the paths has changed,
    not raked, not smoothed,
    each is a dare: follow me.

The walls show signs of cracking,
and the key has rusted in the lock.

Dragon Child (Conversation #2)

(I could teach you.)

Teach me what, Dragon Child?

*(Music, songs, swirling through the air
to fade in the high heavens.)*

Songs. Minor kindlers of artificial fires,
tempting passions ephemeral and unknowable,
until we don't know ourselves.

*(Movement, then, the rhythm of the flame
when it dances over the hearth log.)*

Iridescent scales flash as you sway
in dancing firelight. But I have no scales to flash.

*(Of colour, none. A line drawing
awaiting the child's crayon.)*

I have no need of colour, Dragon Child,
or swaying dance to kindling songs.

*(Well, flight: streaking gray as the clouds
before the vaporous sun.)*

And going where? Here is good enough,
or should be.
Vertiginous loops and dives – no, I'll take
solid grasp on solid ground.

(Well, what then?)

If you would teach me,
if you must teach me…

(What, then?)

I fear to ask.

(Tell me.)

Teach me, Dragon Child.
Teach me

        to

           breathe

              fire.

The Components

There's magic in the components.

Play the chord as an arpeggio,
    hear each note tremble in the air.
Consider the flour, the butter, the eggs,
    before considering the pancakes.
Admire the petals, one by one,
    each essential to the grace of the gardenia.
Taste the tea, but don't forget
        to admire its amber, to reflect on the curves
        of the teapot.

Broad strokes shape the surface.
The picture's depth arises
    from fine brushwork,
    colours and textures
    unnoticed, but completing the whole.

Study the elegance of the letters
    that create the word on the page,
the pattern of hairs on the cat
    where she changes from white to tabby,
The shape of your hand, its veins and wrinkles,
the veins and wrinkles of the leaf.

Bring awareness to the level of components:
    breath by breath,
    heartbeat by heartbeat.

Live, Live

Live – because not to live is
     to squander what you may not receive again.

Live fiercely. Show life what you're made of.

Let it know that it serves you,
     not the other way around.

Live as if the music of the spheres has cut through you,
shattering you into a thousand songs,
lifting you to the sapphire stars, and beyond.

Live with the structure of self-made decisions
     and self-accepted consequences.
Stand up, at least, when you can't stand tall –
and when you do stand tall,
     be the shoulder that others stand on.

Live. And be grateful for each filled moment,
so that at the end you can say,
I lived as my untrammeled natural self.
I learned her ways, and taught her how to dance.

The Road You Will Take

This is the road you will take
because of the flood
that etched a chasm in your heart's understanding.

This is the road you will take
because all you knew was washed away,
even the way back.

You will take this road
with a new, unfamiliar name, the one
you don't remember to answer to yet.

What's left you is in a bag
to suspend from a stick over your shoulder.

You make your small preparations alone,
your only companion the strange new name
worn like a talisman.

Now go.
You take the first step, the seventh,
the ten thousandth.

Fences

My mind is running on fences,
a row of pickets from here to yon,
as if someone had given them an order:
    March!
and there they go, evenly spaced, equally white,
    Just doing their job.

Not myself a fence-sitter,
 I'm left wondering: am I kept in,
    or kept out?

There's no gate, no stile.
The greener grass beckons, persistently,
no doubt enhanced by the march of white,
the ordered slats that hypnotize,
    keep me from turning around,
from admiring the green world that others,
    those on the other side of the fence,
    would choose, if they could.

To the Drowned Villages

Can you name what was left behind?
A toy, a pot, the car that died in '58;
The wallpaper that you chose on your honeymoon,
the sagging bed where your child was born, and died;
The old chair that wouldn't fit
    on the back of the pickup?

Would you allow these things, now,
    to tell the story of before?

And did you watch the waters rise
    around your history?
Or did you leave in a straight line,
    eyes only on tomorrow,
seeking safety in the nameless future,
    in staying dry?

Naps (Terra #7)

When Terra sleeps, she's beyond
our ability to resist.
Stroking her, we wake her up into languid stretches.

But when Terra sleeps
with her head buried under a paw,
we tiptoe by, respecting the sign:
Do Not Disturb.

At the Labour Day Fair

On the Ferris wheel, I have to ask,
But in what way does this
    contribute to truth?
    Is it even real?
The colour and noise, cotton candy and thrills
don't add up
to any useful reality I know.
The fair – outside of time and place,
it's a gaudy trinket thrown in with fine jewels.

Well, be fair here, you say (with a smirk).
Perhaps there is a reality and truth
in the Ferris wheel.
Perhaps the colour, the noise,
the dust and cotton candy and thrills
are a reminder –
    that it can all be fun,
    not as grim as you want to make it,
    a cheerful excursion through
    a September day.
Perhaps the only purpose
perhaps the all-time best purpose,
is happiness.

Hanged Man

In the shadows, a movement, a sideways shift:
    photos free their images,
    ancient stone animates.
The watcher may fail to perceive,
but the seeker knows, and waits.

In the forgotten box, on a shelf somewhere,
a man hangs suspended
    by one taut leg,
    the other forming an inverted four.

Now.
His time has ripened,
His initiation is at an end.
He flexes his body, rises.
    Freeing his pendant leg,
    he drops lightly to the ground.

The die is cast.
Notice has been served.
Hope lives,
    for the space of a breath.
The hanged man touches the hanging tree,
    a parting salute,
and goes.

No Simple Story

I know,
when our eyes meet across the room,
that this is no simple story.

This is a story of:
      Whose turn to clean the litterbox?
      I'm happy for / furious at / fed up with you.
      Fantastic forehand smash!
      Did you balance the chequebook? (And is there
            any money?)
      Let's go for a walk / to dinner / to Hawaii.
      Just go away and leave me alone.
(I love you.)

It takes years to mix it all
into coherence,
to the place where a look returned,
eyes meeting across the room,
sums it all up,
and nothing more is needed
to complete the whole.

Take Good Care

Think you're not god?
Think again.
Are you not the one
  who sited the seed?
  who birthed the child?
  who kneaded the bread to suppleness?

The evidence is in: no other god, transcendent,
will come along and fix things up
  on demand.

Think you're not a destructive god?
Think again.
What of:
  pulling up the dandelion?
  sending the army to pull the trigger?
  the instant and unexpected
    annihilation by flyswatter?

Take good care,
for you are god,
and decisions of life and death are,
  daily,
  yours.
And nothing you do, or want, or pray for,
can separate what you do
from the unfoldment of the whole.

The Hunter

Once he lay in wait,
with cruelty and traps,
ready to snatch
    while the road wound through
    green leaves, wildflowers of summer.

Now, he stalks,
a long way behind, but near enough
that I sense him behind me.
As I kick up the leaves of autumn
    that litter my path,
    waiting for the first snows,
He draws nearer with his longer stride,
    clearer vision.

One day I will turn, and there he'll be.
We'll stand and stare,
and we will know each other.

The Thought of Rain

I try to bless the rain.
But after a week of cast iron skies, monotone drizzle,
Pacific Northwest in winter,
it's hard to find a lingering drop of gratitude
for rain.

So, instead...

I bless
the Idea of Rain.
Caressing its lover the earth,
waking her up to lustiness
and fecundity,

and polishing up the equinox path
that leads, as it must,
to April.

Nursery Rhyme

Written for an artist friend's 70th birthday

There was a woman
    – she was known as Old Woman –
    who lived in a shoe.
But as houses go, it didn't fit very well.
It was too tight, it pinched and rubbed,
and on bad days, it smelled.

So the woman took her paints and brushes
and painted the tongue of the shoe.
Painted sun and moon and sky and clouds,
    and a goddess or two,
and she dreamed her dreams beneath her leather sky.

The woman had so many children
    she didn't know what to do.
Her many children, her creations,
    they poked and prodded,
    they pinched and whined,
    because they knew a make-believe sky
    when they saw one.

So the woman took her palette knife
and honed its edges to razor sharpness
and cut away the tongue of the shoe.

And her children, her creations, tumbled free,
    and each one was a star
    and each one was a thought
    and each one was a goddess.

The woman stuck her head out of the shoe
and said, "All right!" and said, "Life, here I come!"
and out she clambered.
And with paint and brushes
and a razor-edged knife to cut away false horizons,
the woman created a world
    created a life
    created her soul.

And cackled, and sometimes wept.
And her children, her creations, flew to her arms,
    and flew away again,
a star, a thought, a goddess.

The woman threw away the too-tight shoe,
and now she was known as New Woman.
And Life embraced her
    in a hug as large as all creation,
    as large as a star, a thought, a goddess,
    as large as a world, a life, a soul.

Life blessed her, and said, "Welcome home."

On Time (Conversation #1)

Clocks don't tick anymore.
They slide and glide, no pace to the day;
the seconds float, on barely connected clouds.

(But clouds obey their own pattern, you say.)

A pattern to clouds? But no intention.

Like time, no rhythm, no meter.
This day could be going forward, backward, sideways,
for all the not-ticking tells us.

(So, we're not moving forward? you ask.)

Oh, yes, forward, despite the clocks and clouds.

For time, here's a green tomato,
on its earth-tethered umbilical cord,
until the day it releases its fire
in juices running down your chin.

For pattern, haunt the shadows, deeper than clouds,
where yearning grows,
dark to dark, night to night,
long to short to long.

For rhythm, match the starling,
that child of sun and shadows,
obeying a beat beyond your knowing.
And when you catch the echo of his rhythm,
place your hand just here, and here.

The First Day

The first day of warm after a cold spring:
tiny daisies flow in torrents down the slope,
    a waterfall rippling in the breeze.
By the creek the skunk cabbage stands proud,
    blazing yellow in the sun
    flaunting its iconic perfume.
Nuthatches honk their cheerful honk
and dandelions congregate, defiantly gold.
No one has stayed inside, it seems,
and the mower growls its benediction
    to the grass.

The Poet Gets Older

I don't know who I am,
I don't know what I look like –
but I know it's not like before.

Efficiency's shot, tasks pile up
until I'm sent into nervous frenzy.
Lose things, forget ingredients,
sleep less when I long for more.

Nevers loom:
I'll never walk the Camino.
Egypt? The pyramids will stand
    without my admiring.

I'll never get another degree
or wear stilettos
or learn to play classical guitar.

I may never balance a chequebook
    (on the first try).
Smart phones speak an alien language.

The compass of my world narrows.
Pushback is futile, but oh yes, I push.

Until ...
    Evening, wine, book ...
Hmm.
Maybe it is possible
to let the accomplishing go to those
with something to accomplish.

Joining

Yes, this basket is heavy, a little.
I try not to mind.
I've been carrying it for a long time,
thinking it was mine.

Here's the thing: I know now,
what's in this basket,
it isn't mine at all,
only mine to give.
To you I offer what it holds.

With your hands, take from my hands,
that tremble
before this simple, holy gesture.

Our hands
in communion,
we play it forward
into the universal circle.

Twelve Weeks

A long time coming –
    she's never been so radiant.
Why is it different when it's a daughter?
At midnight, when demons walk,
I concentrate on all that is amazingly right,
    holding faith with the upside potential.

We know, we who have been there,
that there is no end.
Your life is never separate
    from the child you carry.

I tell the beads, count the octaves,
    send every blessing I know
    to the twelve-week child of my child,
    its privacy sacrificed to ultrasound.

The egg now becoming a child
lived in me once, in my unborn daughter.
The chain is unbroken; this newcomer
touches all our destinies,
heals the breaks in circles,
completes what needed to be completed.

Shorts

Five Crows

Walking down my road,
three curious, two stately:
    family outing.

The Longest Story

You are through the door.
I have let you through the door,
not welcome, not denied.
Now face to face
we can only stare,
like strangers.

Digestive Upset in Iambic Tetrameter

"Incarcerated flatulence" –
a musical, descriptive term.

This afternoon, my abdomen
attempts to sing the harmony.

Seduction

I

She's the one.
Courtship is minimal –
he knows he's irresistible.

II

He looks on, impassive.
The girls huddle together,
sleepy after lunch.

Wide awake, their calves
explore the fertile meadow.

The Diet (Terra #4)

A cat on a diet
     is a pathetic thing
     but has her uses.
From guilt or fellow feeling,
     I've lost five pounds.

Planning Dinner – Terra #6

From behind her window
Terra chitters and twirls her tail.
She longs to explore
the subtle taste distinction
between chickadee and sparrow.

Sandpipers

Sandpipers
reflect on the shiny-wet beach.
Scrabbled tracks write a story
I haven't learned to read.

Their small bodies launch,
and in formation
create an echo wave
over the sea.

Pilgrim Path

*With thanks to David Whyte for his inspirational
thoughts and writings about pilgrims and
pilgrimage.*

Just for today, put your life
    in a new context,
and don the garb of a pilgrim.
Just for today, allow your toes
to curl in the sacred ground
of the path before you.

Allow your eyes to see horizons,
but no clear destination,
and no sense of how to get there,

and take a first step.
And give your full attention to that step.
Tell your mind it need not consider
the obstacles and storms ahead.

The things you thought you wanted –
watch them fall away down the mountainside.
Leave them where they land.

Your job, just for today,
is to take the steps that lead to who knows where,
stripped to fundamentals,
alone on the path.

Cleaning the Liquor Cabinet

She's gone now.
Cleaning the liquor cabinet, I found,
shoved far in the back, an ancient box
of powdered whisky sour mix.

Whisky sours ...

She made them in a small pitcher,
ready when I got home from a summer job.
She at the stove, I at the table, we'd share them
     before supper.

Incongruous, those romantic cocktails
     in the kitchen.
They hinted at something that wasn't.
At memories – of hotel ballrooms,
     camellias, corsages and beaux.
At possibilities, dreams of successes and one day love.
Two women, two sets of dreams, meshed
in the nightly ritual of whisky sours.

Three packets left.
Rock hard now, after thirty years.
I'd have liked to mix them into
     the last jiggers of Jim Beam,
raise a toast to that last shared summer.

Flyboys

In the war he remembers so well, my father fought
the Hump of the Himalayas:
>> jungle, weather, altitude,
>> strafing from the Japanese.
Air Transport Command, twin engine props,
Distinguished Flying Cross
>> mounted in a frame on the wall.

For years they got together,
these Hump pilots,
until the few that remained were too old.
They hardly know their country anymore –
>> only to be expected, seventy years on.
Still, they'd love to stand and salute, they'd love
>> to be called once again.

When you read the history, you find
>> monsoons and bugs,
>> inedible food and soggy sheets,
>> a tiger on the path,
>> and too many planes falling out of the sky,
>> lost to the mountains.
But as it lives in the hearts of these flyboys,
>> it was great adventure, the greatest honour.
They were there; they did this once.

Whatever the world has come round to be,
whatever we think of the glory of war,
let us acknowledge these old men, their simple pride,
their war a standing symbol
>> of what matters.

Prayer

The best prayers have no words.
They unfold with no warning
when the sanctity and need of the day
drive inward, to the temple
kept ready in the deepest heart.

The best prayers cannot be spoken.
There are no words for a hawk in the sun,
for the loss of a mother.

Because no words are needed.
The heart is wiser than we are,
and creates its own language.

Spring Garden

I remember spring back east, an ugly time:
    damp cold and frozen mud,
    dirty snow in patches,
    gutters blocked with ice, and icy puddles.

And always through the ugliness,
    a brave and perfect purple crocus
    knowing better than the weather
    what the season is.

Elder Reflection

If I had the fiery strength of twenty
I'd have caught the mailman
and you'd have had your birthday card on time.

If I had the lean, spare strength of forty
the pickle jar would not have been the stronger,
and lunch would have had more zest.

But what am I talking about, anyway?

The mail*person* brings nothing personal,
and arthritic hands use tools to defeat pickle jars.
Twenty and forty look at me, bewildered.

Just more of the wonders of aging, right?
Counting blessings is mandatory,
gets us through the letterless deliveries,
the tang-less lunches.

Perspective

My friend delights in ordinary things:

The nine-pound turkey
when the rest are twenty-two;
a glass of wine to toast
the overstayed aunt's departing;
a shower, warmth, clean hair
when the power comes back on;
the unexpected lift on a snowy day;
the blessed relief of a backache gone.

My friend delights, and finds delight,
and speaks delight.

And I speak ... what?
not quite delight?
Of course I *can* ...
I just have to ...

okay,
yes,
I get it.

First Trip Abroad

I rode around on the bus and saw the sights,
ate the couscous, admired the pouring of the tea,
    the goats' heads and exotic trinkets in the souk.

Then we stopped for gas, and that was when I saw it,
the sign, the name of the station:
    Afriquia.

Africa.

I stood on the solid ground outside the station,
almost quivering with gut-level awareness
that this really, really, isn't Canada.

You Have the Use

You have the use of your arms
    (somehow, in clouds of thought).
Take up, then, your pail and rag.
Polish the window to invisibility.
Invite the heavens to throw a path of sunbeam,
    unimpeded,
      onto your floor.
Watch, as the path's beginning
migrates across the textures of the carpet.

You have the use of your legs
    (though none might know).
Flex, then, the long muscles,
stalk the sunbeam on the floor.
Set off at a walk or run,
(once you pin down the beginning)
and seek the far end of the path,
the end that vanishes into dreams.

You have the use of your dreams
    (and how many do not?).
Pursue tomorrow if you dare,
but remember the sun that moves across the floor,
the path dissolving ahead in brilliance.
Remember that tomorrow is not today,
and you can't say where tomorrow will be,
or even, with certainty, where you started from.

You have the use of the future
      (do not we all?).
You have the potency of dreams
and sunbeams,
the lure of the path you gave entrance to
with rag and pail,
the path your muscles yearn to follow
into the sun.

On Hearing Sacred Chant

I

The notes of chant are embodied things,
soaring into the sanctuary vault,
into the vault of heaven,
each note sailing its own vibration,
navigating in a holy silence,
the sum a resonance beyond mere music.

II

Silence shapes the space,
binding and defining,
binding me to the notes,
this mystery of sanctity.

III

Harmony looses a flood of them
in glorious formation,
congregating below the arc
of stars and chapel
above me, resonating down,
teaching the way to fly.

IV

White they are,
like a thousand angels overhead.

V

The words could be anything,
in my language or another,
or no language at all.
It all translates to the same heartsong:

　　Come away home.

The notes and the silent spaces carry the message.
The white angels carry the message:

　　Come away home.
　　Come away home.

The Hummingbird

The cat caught a hummingbird today.
Under two seconds from doze to attack,
a clean kill.

I took the tiny husk away,
    its iridescence already lost,
    its beak a useless black toothpick,
and placed it under the dense ivy
to continue its earthly work in peace.

Tonight the cat seems more than usually assured.
Her first kill – she has fulfilled
some innate destiny of her own.

But I am haunted
by the spirit of hummingbird.
Beauty, acrobatics, curiosity: life,
snatched away in two raw seconds.
I would undo that moment
if it were mine to recover.

The cat stretches in the evening sun,
content in the rightness of her world.

Psalm: In Place

Flowers never question their place
on the fertile earth.
The daffodil, out in the cold spring rain,
just gets on with it – living, that is.

My hands doubt -
    tell me, show me, my life, my role.
I ask that the cold rain
not discourage me.

Rock is solid
in its siting on the earth.
The stone, even tumbling down the river,
knows its place and roots there
until the next shaking.

My feet doubt -
    tell me, show me, my life, my path.
I ask that the tumbling stream
not disorient me.

As I go forth
May the sure wisdom of the daffodil be mine,
may the certain anchor of the stone be mine.

May the earth be mine,
foundation and fundament.
May I walk its surface, hold its bounty;
in this certainty
may I go forth.

Missing (Terra #8)

Terra's disappeared.
We've scoured the house – no trace.
She'll turn up in her own good time.

Resigned, we go about our day,
wondering where she hides, wanting her here with us.

But Terra keeps her secrets.
Inscrutable, she isn't telling.

From an Older Sister

They say, when you were six months old,
you and she would stare into
each other's eyes
forever,
blue on blue,

as if hypnotized, or adoring.

No wonder I believed
she loved you best.

Waiting for the Snow

In the forecast: snow beginning overnight,
tapering off tomorrow morning,
total accumulation ten centimeters.

I check the window again:
        black, no snow.

I've read as much as I want to.
Blues on the radio, suitable
for a snowy Saturday night.
I concoct a cocoa, stir in Cointreau.

(I want this snow.)

The gas fire burns sedately, no dynamic
        flares and crackles.

I've almost finished the crossword -
        or at least, I'm stumped,
        so let's say it's finished,
until tomorrow when everything will be changed.

When the brown world will be purified.

I don't want it to happen without me.
If transformation is the game, I want to play.

I've bored the cat; she's asleep.

(Why doesn't it start?)

I could lose at solitaire, pick up another book …

(I'm waiting.)

Easy enough to wake up to snow.
I want to be with it when it fills the night,
        the first quiet flakes
        then thicker and thicker, sticking,
        paradigm shifting.
Changing midnight into miracle.

(Please snow.)

The Nor'wester (Misty #2)

(The Nor'wester is a weather pattern of strong, hot northwesterly winds found around Christchurch, New Zealand. When it blows for days on end they say it can drive you mad.)

Camellias chase the cat,
>red play-balls tipped with brown
>go bounding helter-skelter on the lawn.

Cat, made feral by relentless wind
>attacks with a mighty somersault,
>then bolts.

If there were some hiding place,
senses wouldn't mind so much
>the shrieking cracks in windowsills,
>laundry static-crackly wrapped around the line,
>heavy-hearted vacuums in the gaps
>where buildings split the rushing air.

Cat, under the camellia,
>crouches, submissive,
>cries to the nor'wester.

Thoughts on Growing Older

This aging business would be easier
if the clouds would stop layering
    shades of gray against gray.
And if only the birds that frequent the feeder
      would sing – but it's not their season for singing.
And if only the leaves that fall from the pin oak
      would do it all at once
      instead of leaf by leaf all winter,
      like a reminder.
And if only routine were shaken somehow,
breakfast weren't the other half
    of yesterday's grapefruit ...

And if only insomniac nights were less haunted
    by fifty-year-old rock and roll.

To Sherry, on a Wet Winter Day

The still image:
liquid perfection in a flawless container.
No sheeting inside
  or lip-formed crescent on the rim –
  just deep, clear amber.
So still, it might be glass within the glass.

This small, pure vessel
  captures summer's lyric,
  memories cast where no reality intrudes.

I lift. I sip. The sun returns.

Shrinkage

My soul tore itself from my chest, saying,
What you have become is too small to contain
    what you might be.
Your sprouted wings have atrophied with the years.
Where the winds dance into the future
    you falter and fall.

Look, just once, behind that tight
    and frightened spirit.
And when you do, be extravagant.
Blessings can be counted, if you must, like talents,
    tallied up for the accounting,
but how much better
    to give them wing,
    and let them fly.

Familiar (Haricat #1)

Because you're small and dainty, I assume
    you can't take care of yourself.
Because you wear a long and glossy
    coat of many colours,
    I think you must be vulnerable.
Because you sleep curled up by the fire
and find such satisfaction in the cleaning of a face,
    I assume you need me.

I notice that you make no similar assumptions
    about me.

You want none of my protection.
Life's a dare. And you're not afraid.

It runs, you chase it.
It smells like food, you eat.
It goes up, you climb,
    and think later about getting down.
It tires you out, you find a warm, safe place,
    and purr yourself to sleep.
If it kills you, well,
    so what?

Can it possibly be so simple?
Wisdom of cat: innate, pure,
without analysis,
deceptively straightforward.

The Call

When your yearning is as deep
as Spirit's longing for you,
    that's Faith,
a mutual need and attraction,
deeply intimate,
an antiphon for the soul's return home.

(A tribute to the words of John O'Donohue)

Alphabetical List of Titles

About The Author

Elizabeth Carson lives and writes in Victoria, British Columbia.

To learn more about her life and work, please visit lizanncarson.com.